ADHD Warrior

ADHD Warrior: Helping Children Conquer ADHD Unwanted Behaviors

Published by Gatekeeper Press
7853 Gunn Hwy, Suite 209.
Tampa, FL 33626
www.GatekeeperPress.com

Library of Congress Control Number: 2021949207

ISBN (hardcover): 9781662921414
ISBN (paperback): 9781662921421
eISBN: 9781662921438

ADHD Warrior

Helping Children Conquer ADHD Unwanted Behaviors

Written by
Dr. Ambroes Pass-Turner

gatekeeper press
Tampa, Florida

Roxie, you will always have
a special place in my heart.
You are truly missed.

My name is Roxie. I am a happy 8-year-old girl who enjoys running around the yard with my dog Nora, spending time with my family, playing with friends, and learning.

Mother took me to see the doctor because I am having issues with concentrating and focusing during school. The doctor informed mother that I have ADHD. "ADHD" stands for attention-deficit/hyperactivity disorder. ADHD doesn't stop me from doing the things that I enjoy. It is nothing to be ashamed of. Many children with ADHD find that their symptoms decrease or disappear as they get older.

Mom and Dad decided not to put me on medication. Even with medication, it is important for children to learn healthy coping skills to control ADHD. Every day I face challenges.

Sometimes, I have difficulty paying attention. At school my mind wanders, and I daydream of being a princess in a faraway land. This distracts me and prevents me from listening to the teacher.

At times, I am very disorganized. My book bag is always messy, which causes me to lose things. Mother and I spent the entire weekend completing homework. When it was time to turn the homework in, I could not find it in my book bag. But I know that I saw Mother place it in there.

Sitting still is a major problem for me.
I must have gotten out of my seat at least ten times
today during class to sharpen my pencil.

After completing classwork, I become so bored that I tap on my desk or squirm in my seat.

I often feel restless and on edge.

Yesterday, while in the lunch line, I pulled Devin's hair and had to eat lunch at the teachers' table.

Waiting for my turn to speak is so hard to do.

I blurt out answers and interrupt others.

In class, I am overly talkative and struggle to be quiet.

I make careless mistakes.

Last night, I left the faucet running after brushing my teeth.

Staying on task is difficult. If the doorbell rings while I am cleaning my room. I forget all about cleaning.

I feel like no one understands or believes me when I say, "I forgot," or "I can't help it."

My parents are always getting on me for forgetting or not paying attention, so I lose my computer and phone privileges a lot.

My parents came up with some great ideas to help me better manage my ADHD.

They established structure at home because children with ADHD do their best when they know what to expect.

They changed my diet, limiting my intake of sweets and processed foods. These days, my diet consists of more gluten-free foods and fresh vegetables.

Mom and I created an ADHD Focus Plan. She asked me to write down a task that I need to do. I wrote "clean my room."

She suggested that the task be broken down into smaller parts, so I wrote "make my bed."

Next, we made a schedule for making my bed. I will make my bed every morning when I wake up.

Then, we set a reminder to help me remember. I taped the words "make my bed" on my bed so that I can see it every morning.

The items needed to make my bed are already present in the morning. When it is time for me to change the sheets on my bed, Mom places the fresh sheets in the chair next to the bed so that I can see them.

I feel a sense of accomplishment every morning after making my bed.

Knowing my objectives helps me stay on task and not be distracted.

At home, there are routines for homework, meals, playing, bedtime, and preparing for school.

My parents have created a simple list of rules for me. If I complete my homework or chores but forget to complete one of my other tasks, they focus on the accomplishment rather than the mistake.

I have a studying routine that consists of studying for one hour after school. We have a dedicated study area for me. The room is free of distractions. Study materials are in the room so that I don't spend time searching for what I need to get my work done.

Participating in soccer has helped with my ADHD. Playing on the soccer team is fun, burns energy, and develops my social skills.

My parents and teachers have a good relationship. They work together to make sure that ADHD symptoms do not interfere with my education.

The teacher moved my desk to the front of the class so she can intervene if she notices me getting off task.

I am always receiving praise for good behavior. This encourages me. I understand that there are consequences for negative behavior.

Practicing these coping skills at home has improved my unwanted behavior at school.

Having ADHD is not fun but controlling it on my own is a good feeling. So, I practice self-control and awareness.

When I fall short, I remember that perfection is an unrealistic expectation and I continue to do my best.

Dr. Ambroes Pass-Turner Tips

1. If you can't find behavior worth praising, compliment children on extended periods without unwanted behavior.

....

2. Rewards are more effective than punishment to motivate children.

....

3. Try not to over punish. Children don't usually remember why they are grounded after two weeks.

....

4. Homework hour reduces the chance of children forgetting or avoiding homework.

....

5. Please remember that "perfection is an unrealistic expectation."

ADHD WARRIOR

CERTIFICATE OF ACHIEVEMENT

This certificate certifies that _____ has demonstrated outstanding self-control in improving unwanted behaviors associated with attention-deficit/hyperactivity disorder (ADHD) or attention-deficit disorder (ADD).

Dr. Ambraes Pass-Turner

Presenter

About the Author

Dr. Ambroes Pass-Turner is a Doctor of Counseling Psychology, and the owner of APT Counseling Services, LLC. She is also a psychotherapist, professor, published author, and scholar-practitioner. Dr. Ambroes Pass-Turner has published the books *Rex's Journey: Helping Children Understand and Cope with Emotions* and *Childhood Sexual Abuse: Pathway to Mental Health Issues and Delinquent Behavior.* She is the founder of Dr. Ambroes Kids Corner, a YouTube channel that addresses children's behavior and mental health concerns. Her dissertation research topic was "Women Offenders Perception of Cognitive Behavioral Therapy Interventions in Treating Childhood Sexual Abuse: Implication for Treatment." She is a subject matter expert on the topics "Why some survivors minimize their abuse: When this coping mechanism can be a good thing" and "How survivors' advocates can avoid burnout" with National publication agency Domestic Shelters. Dr. Ambroes Pass-Turner has been inducted into the prestigious Marquis Who's Who Biographical Registry and recognized for her expertise as a counselor. Dr. Pass-Turner holds credentials as a Licensed Professional Counselor, Certified Professional Counselor Supervisor, Doctoral addictions Counselor, Master Addictions Counselor, Board Certified Professional Counselor, Board Certified Telemental Health Provider, National Certified Counselor, Certified Clinical Mental Health Counselor, Clinically Certified Human Trafficking Victims Services Provider, Clinically Certified Domestic Violence Counselor, and Clinically Certified Forensic Counselor. She is a member of the American Counseling Association, Licensed Professional Counselor Association of Georgia, American Psychological Association, National Board for Certified Counselors, National Association of Forensic Counselors, and Delta Sigma Theta Sorority, Inc.